My Quran Journey

More than a Journal

Belongs to:_____

© 2018 by Amna Farooq

"In the name of Allah, most Gracious, most Compassionate"

Assalaamu 'Alaikum Wa Rahmatullahi Wa Barakatuh

وَنَزَّلْنَا
عَلَيْكَ الْكِتَابَ تِبْيَانًا لِّكُلِّ شَيْءٍ وَهُدًى وَرَحْمَةً وَبُشْرَىٰ لِلْمُسْلِمِينَ

"And We have sent down to you the Book as clarification for all things and as guidance and mercy and good tidings for the Muslims" [16:89]

This journal aims to facilitate your learning journey with the Holy Quran. You can document your thoughts and reflections, explore meanings and make connections to develop a deeper understanding of the Holy Quran.

The journal has been divided into two main sections with study plans to learn ayahs individually, and surahs as a whole. It provides you an opportunity to track your study progress with help of various charts and trackers.

In addition, it has an interesting facts sheet about the Holy Quran and incorporates a collection of 30 important duas from the Quran in the first section.

It features:

- Quran facts
- 30 duas from Quran
- Ayah study plan
- Surah study plan
- New Vocabulary chart
- Monthly review
- Weekly review
- Quran tracker

Understanding the only book of Allah is something we owe to ourselves as believers, but most importantly, we owe it to Allah (SWT). May Allah (SWT) guide as to the truth and enlighten our journey in understanding The Holy Quran. (Allahumma Ameen)

Quranic Facts

Do You Know ?

The Holy Quran has 30 parts and 114 surahs.

The literal meaning of Quran is "that which is being read".

Prophet Muhammad (PBUH) was 40 years old when the first verse of Quran was revealed to Him (PBUH)

The revelation started in the Holy month of Ramadan.

Bismillah Al-Rahman Al-Raheem is repeated 114 times in the Quran.

All except for Surat "Al Tawbah" start with Bismillah al-Rahman al-Raheem.

Surat "Al Namel, No. 27" has Bismillah Al-Rahman Al-Raheem in its body

Al-Baqarah is the longest surah in the Quran

Al-Kawthar is the shortest surah in the Quran

Surat Al-Ikhlas is considered 1/3 of the Quran (Sahih Muslim)

Quran was revealed over 23 years: 13 in Makkah and 10 in Madina

Surat Al-Dahr was revealed in respect to Ahlul Bayt (P)

The word Quran is used 70 times in the Holy Quran.

The first Surah in Quran, Surah Al-Fatiha is known as the Mother of Quran or Ummul Quran. (At-Tirmidhi)

6 Surahs or chapters in Quran are named after Prophets who came before Prophet Muhammad (PBUH).

Quran has other names also, which are:

Al-Huda (The Guidance), Al-Dhikr (The Reminder), Al-Furqan (The Criterion-for judging right from wrong), Al-Shifa (The Healing), Al-Mau`iza (The Admonition), Al-Rahmah (The Mercy), Al-Nur (The Light), Al-Haqq (The Truth), and Al-Burhaan (The Clear Argument).

Prophet Muhammad (PBUH) used to revise the verses of Quran with Angel Jibril every year. In the year before his death, Prophet Muhammad (PBUH) revised Quran with Jibril twice.

The Qur'an will be a proof for us on the Day of Judgment.

The Qur'an will intercede for us on the Day of Judgment.

Your status in this life will be raised.

You will be from the best of the people.

There are ten rewards for each letter you recite from the Qur'an.

The reciters of the Qur'an will be in the company of the angels.

Your position in Paradise is determined by the portion of Qur'an you memorize in this life!

The Qur'an will lead you to Paradise!

Rewards of reciting/learning Quran

More Facts

There are 20 surahs of the Quran that are Madni whereas, 82 surahs are Makki. The remaining surahs (12) are subject to a difference of opinion between the honourable 'Ulama (scholars). These 12 are Surah Al-Fatihah, Surah Ar-Ra'ad, Surah as-Swaff, At-Taghaabun, Al-Mutafiffeen, Al-Qadr, al-Bayyinah, az-Zilzaal, Surah At-Tawheed (Al-Ikhlas), Al-Falaq and An-Naas.

Characteristics of Makki and Madni surah

Makki Surahs

1. Before the Hijrah.
2. Strong/harsh words.
3. Shorter Ayyat.
4. Powerful impact, proofs and arguments.
5. Focus on Tawheed.
6. Focus on stories of previous Prophets.

Madni Surahs

1. After the Hijrah.
2. Gentle style of address.
3. Longer Ayyat.
4. Mention of rulings without proofs and reasoning.
5. Detailed rulings concerning acts of worship and transaction.
6. Themes concerning Jews, Christians and Munafiqeen.

Important mentions in the Quran

The best drink mentioned in the Quran is Milk.
The best food to eat, mentioned in the Quran is Honey.
The best month among all months is mentioned as Ramadan in the Quran.
The best night mentioned in the Quran is Laylatul Qadr.
The name Muhammad is mentioned 4 times in the Holy Quran.
25 Prophets are mentioned by name in the Quran.
Friday is the only day of week that is mentioned in the Quran.
There are 5 mosques mentioned in Holy Quran,three directly by name,
Masjid-ul-Haram(2:150), Masjid-ul-Aqsa (17:1), Masjid ul Zarrar(9:107).The other two
are mentioned indirectly not by name, Masjid ul Quba(9:108), Masjid ul Nabawi(18:21)

GUIDANCE

ذَٰلِكَ الْكِتَابُ لَا رَيْبَ فِيهِ هُدًى لِّلْمُتَّقِينَ

This is the Book of Allah, there is no doubt in it; it is a guidance for the pious. (2:2)

تِلْكَ آيَاتُ الْكِتَابِ الْحَكِيمِ هُدًى وَرَحْمَةً لِّلْمُحْسِنِينَ

These are the verses of the Book of wisdom. These are a guidance and mercy for the righteous. (31:3)

إِنَّ هَٰذَا الْقُرْآنَ يَهْدِي لِلَّتِي هِيَ أَقْوَمُ وَيُبَشِّرُ الْمُؤْمِنِينَ الَّذِينَ يَعْمَلُونَ الصَّالِحَاتِ أَنَّ لَهُمْ أَجْرًا كَبِيرًا

Surely this Qur'an guides to the Way which is perfectly straight and gives the good news to the believers who do good that they shall have a magnificent reward. (17:9)

Ayah Study

Study Plan

1. Write the ayah with translation.
2. Look into the context of the ayah, within the passage and Surah.
3. Record a brief commentary from your favorite resource.
4. Reflect, and jot down your own thoughts and understanding about the Ayah.
5. Figure out how you can implement what you have learned.
6. Learn the key words and write down the meanings.

بِسْمِ اللَّهِ الرَّحْمَنِ الرَّحِيمِ

Date:_____

Day:_____

Ayah Tracker

Juz: _____

Surah: _____

Ayah No: _____

Progress Record

Studied: ☐

Memorised: ☐

Revised: ☐

Ayah:

Context:

Brief Commentary:

Source:

My Understanding:

words/meaning

How can I implement the lessons in my life?

رَبَّنَا تَقَبَّلْ مِنَّا إِنَّكَ أَنتَ السَّمِيعُ الْعَلِيمُ

" O our Lord ! accept (this service) from us, verily You and You (alone) are the Hearer, the Knower"
Surah Al-Baqrah
verse 127

ADDITIONAL NOTES:

بِسْمِ اللَّهِ الرَّحْمَنِ الرَّحِيمِ

Date:_____   Day:_____

Ayah Tracker

Juz: _____
Surah: _____
Ayah No: _____

Progress Record

Studied: ☐
Memorised: ☐
Revised: ☐

Ayah:

Context:

Brief Commentary:

Source:

My Understanding:

words/meaning

How can I implement the lessons in my life?

رَبَّنَا لَا تُؤَاخِذْنَا إِن نَّسِينَا أَوْ أَخْطَأْنَا رَبَّنَا وَلَا تَحْمِلْ عَلَيْنَا إِصْرًا كَمَا
حَمَلْتَهُ عَلَى الَّذِينَ مِن قَبْلِنَا

Our Lord ! take us not to task if we forget or fall into error. Our Lord! Lay not upon us such a burden as You did lay upon those before us

Surah Al-Baqarah ,verse 286

ADDITIONAL NOTES:

Date:_____   Day:_____

Ayah Tracker

Juz: _____

Surah: _____

Ayah No: _____

Progress Record

Studied: ☐

Memorised: ☐

Revised: ☐

Ayah:

Context:

Brief Commentary:

Source:

My Understanding:

words/meaning

How can I implement the lessons in my life?

رَبَّنَا وَلَا تُحَمِّلْنَا مَا لَا طَاقَةَ لَنَا بِهِ ۖ وَاعْفُ عَنَّا وَاغْفِرْ لَنَا وَارْحَمْنَا ۚ أَنتَ مَوْلَانَا فَانصُرْنَا عَلَى الْقَوْمِ الْكَافِرِينَ

Our Lord! Lay not upon us such a burden as You did lay upon those before us. Our Lord! Impose not on us that which we have not the strength to bear, grant us forgiveness and have mercy on us. You are our Protector. Help us against those who deny the truth.
Surah Al Baqrah , verse 286

16

ADDITIONAL NOTES:

بِسْمِ اللَّهِ الرَّحْمَٰنِ الرَّحِيمِ

Date:_____   Day:_____

Ayah Tracker

Juz: _____

Surah: _____

Ayah No: _____

Progress Record

Studied: ☐

Memorised: ☐

Revised: ☐

Ayah:

Context:

Brief Commentary:

Source:

My Understanding:

words/meaning

How can I implement the lessons in my life?

رَبَّنَا إِنَّنَا آمَنَّا فَاغْفِرْ لَنَا ذُنُوبَنَا وَقِنَا عَذَابَ النَّارِ

"Our Lord ! surely we believe, therefore forgive us our faults and save us from the punishment of the fire"

Surah Al Imran, verse 16

ADDITIONAL NOTES:

بِسْمِ اللَّهِ الرَّحْمَنِ الرَّحِيمِ

Date:_____   Day:_____

Ayah Tracker

Juz: _____

Surah: _____

Ayah No: _____

Progress Record

Studied: ☐

Memorised: ☐

Revised: ☐

Ayah:

Context:

Brief Commentary:

Source:

My Understanding:

words/meaning

How can I implement the lessons in my life?

رَبَّنَا اغْفِرْ لَنَا ذُنُوبَنَا وَ إِسْرَافَنَا فِي أَمْرِنَا وَ ثَبِّتْ أَقْدَامَنَا وَ انصُرْنَا عَلَى الْقَوْمِ الْكَافِرِينَ

"Our Lord ! forgive us our sins and our transgressions, establish our feet firmly and help us against the disbelieving people"
Surah Al Imran, verse 147

Additional Notes:

بِسْمِ اللَّهِ الرَّحْمَنِ الرَّحِيمِ

Date:_____   Day:_____

Ayah Tracker

Juz: _____
Surah: _____
Ayah No: _____

Progress Record

Studied: ☐

Memorised: ☐

Revised: ☐

Ayah:

Context:

Brief Commentary:

Source:

My Understanding:

words/meaning

How can I implement the lessons in my life?

رَبَّنَا ظَلَمْنَا أَنفُسَنَا وَإِن لَّمْ تَغْفِرْ لَنَا وَتَرْحَمْنَا لَنَكُونَنَّ مِنَ الْخَاسِرِينَ

"Our Lord! We have wronged ourselves. If You forgive us not, and bestow not upon us Your Mercy, we shall certainly be of the losers."
Surah al Ar'af, verse 23

ADDITIONAL NOTES:

بِسْمِ اللَّهِ الرَّحْمَنِ الرَّحِيمِ

Date:_____   Day:_____

Ayah Tracker

Juz: _____
Surah: _____
Ayah No: _____

Progress Record

Studied: ☐

Memorised: ☐

Revised: ☐

Ayah:

Context:

Brief Commentary:

Source:

My Understanding:

words/meaning

How can I implement the lessons in my life?

رَبِّ إِنِّي لِمَا أَنْزَلْتَ إِلَيَّ مِنْ خَيْرٍ فَقِيرٌ

"My Lord! Truly, I am in need of whatever good that You send down to me!"

Surah Al Qasas, verse 24

ADDITIONAL NOTES:

بِسْمِ اللَّهِ الرَّحْمَنِ الرَّحِيمِ

Date: _____   Day: _____

Ayah Tracker

Juz: _____
Surah: _____
Ayah No: _____

Progress Record

Studied: ☐
Memorised: ☐
Revised: ☐

Ayah:

Context:

Brief Commentary:

Source:

My Understanding:

words/meaning

How can I implement the lessons in my life?

رَّبِّ أَعُوذُ بِكَ مِنْ هَمَزَاتِ الشَّيَاطِينِ وَأَعُوذُ بِكَ رَبِّ أَن يَحْضُرُونِ

"My Lord! I seek refuge in You from (the) suggestions (of) the evil ones, And I seek refuge with You, My Lord, lest they may attend (or come near) me."
Surah Al Mu'minun, verse 97-98

ADDITIONAL NOTES:

بِسْمِ اللَّهِ الرَّحْمَـٰنِ الرَّحِيمِ

Date:_____   Day:_____

Ayah Tracker

Juz: _____
Surah: _____
Ayah No: _____

Progress Record
Studied: ☐
Memorised: ☐
Revised: ☐

Ayah:

Context:

Brief Commentary:

Source:

My Understanding:

words/meaning

How can I implement the lessons in my life?

فَاطِرَ السَّمَاوَاتِ وَالْأَرْضِ أَنتَ وَلِيِّي فِي الدُّنْيَا وَالْآخِرَةِ تَوَفَّنِي مُسْلِمًا وَأَلْحِقْنِي بِالصَّالِحِينَ

"The (only) Creator of the heavens and the earth ! You are my Wali (Protector, Helper, Supporter, Guardian, etc.) in this world and in the Hereafter, cause me to die as a Muslim (the one submitting to Your Will), and join me with the righteous."

Surah Yusuf, verse 101

ADDITIONAL NOTES:

بِسْمِ اللَّهِ الرَّحْمَنِ الرَّحِيمِ

Date:_____   Day:_____

Ayah Tracker

Juz: _____
Surah: _____
Ayah No: _____

Progress Record

Studied: ☐
Memorised: ☐
Revised: ☐

Ayah:

Context:

Brief Commentary:

Source:

My Understanding:

words/meaning

How can I implement the lessons in my life?

لَّا إِلَهَ إِلَّا أَنتَ سُبْحَانَكَ إِنِّي كُنتُ مِنَ الظَّالِمِينَ

"(There is) no god except You, Glory be to You! Indeed, I have been of the wrongdoers."
Surah Al Anbiya, verse 87

ADDITIONAL NOTES:

بِسْمِ اللَّهِ الرَّحْمَنِ الرَّحِيمِ

Date:_____   Day:_____

Ayah Tracker

Juz: _____
Surah: _____
Ayah No: _____

Progress Record

Studied: ☐
Memorised: ☐
Revised: ☐

Ayah:

Context:

Brief Commentary:

Source:

My Understanding:

words/meaning

How can I implement the lessons in my life?

رَبِّ هَبْ لِي حُكْمًا وَأَلْحِقْنِي بِالصَّالِحِينَ

"My Lord! Grant me authority and join me with the righteous."
Surah Ash Shu'ara, verse 83

ADDITIONAL NOTES:

بِسْمِ اللَّهِ الرَّحْمَٰنِ الرَّحِيمِ

Date: _____   Day: _____

Ayah Tracker

Juz: _____
Surah: _____
Ayah No: _____

Progress Record

Studied: ☐
Memorised: ☐
Revised: ☐

Ayah:

Context:

Brief Commentary:

Source:

My Understanding:

words/meaning

How can I implement the lessons in my life?

رَبَّنَا أَفْرِغْ عَلَيْنَا صَبْرًا وَتَوَفَّنَا مُسْلِمِينَ

"Our Lord! pour out on us patience, and cause us to die as Muslims."
Surah Al Ar'af, verse 126

ADDITIONAL NOTES:

بِسْمِ اللَّهِ الرَّحْمَنِ الرَّحِيمِ

Date:_____   Day:_____

Ayah Tracker

Juz: _____

Surah: _____

Ayah No: _____

Progress Record

Studied: ☐

Memorised: ☐

Revised: ☐

Ayah:

Context:

Brief Commentary:

Source:

My Understanding:

words/meaning

How can I implement the lessons in my life?

رَبِّ ابْنِ لِي عِندَكَ بَيْتًا فِي الْجَنَّةِ

"My Lord, build for me near You a house in Paradise."
Surah At Tahrim, verse 11

ADDITIONAL NOTES:

47

بِسْمِ اللَّهِ الرَّحْمَنِ الرَّحِيمِ

Date:_____   Day:_____

Ayah Tracker

Juz: _____
Surah: _____
Ayah No: _____

Progress Record

Studied: ☐
Memorised: ☐
Revised: ☐

Ayah:

Context:

Brief Commentary:

Source:

My Understanding:

words/meaning

How can I implement the lessons in my life?

رَبَّنَا اغْفِرْ لِي وَلِوَالِدَيَّ وَلِلْمُؤْمِنِينَ يَوْمَ يَقُومُ الْحِسَابُ

"Our Lord! Forgive me and my parents, and (all) the believers on the Day when the reckoning will be established."
Surah Ibrahim, verse 41

ADDITIONAL NOTES:

بِسْمِ اللَّهِ الرَّحْمَنِ الرَّحِيمِ

Date:_____   Day:_____

Ayah Tracker

Juz: _____

Surah: _____

Ayah No: _____

Progress Record

Studied: ☐

Memorised: ☐

Revised: ☐

Ayah:

Context:

Brief Commentary:

Source:

My Understanding:

words/meaning

How can I implement the lessons in my life?

رَبَّنَا مَا خَلَقْتَ هَـٰذَا بَاطِلًا سُبْحَانَكَ فَقِنَا عَذَابَ النَّارِ

" Our Rabb! You have not created this in vain. Glory to You! Save us from the punishment of Fire."
Surah Al Imran, verse 191

ADDITIONAL NOTES:

بِسْمِ اللَّهِ الرَّحْمَٰنِ الرَّحِيمِ

Date:_____   Day:_____

Ayah Tracker

Juz: _____

Surah: _____

Ayah No: _____

Progress Record

Studied: ☐

Memorised: ☐

Revised: ☐

Ayah:

Context:

Brief Commentary:

Source:

My Understanding:

words/meaning

How can I implement the lessons in my life?

رَبَّنَا لَا تَجْعَلْنَا مَعَ الْقَوْمِ الظَّالِمِينَ

''Our Lord ! place us not with the wrongdoing people''
Surah Al Ar'af, verse 47

ADDITIONAL NOTES:

بِسْمِ اللَّهِ الرَّحْمَنِ الرَّحِيمِ

Date:_____   Day:_____

Ayah Tracker

Juz: _____

Surah: _____

Ayah No: _____

Progress Record

Studied: ☐

Memorised: ☐

Revised: ☐

Ayah:

Context:

Brief Commentary:

Source:

My Understanding:

words/meaning

How can I implement the lessons in my life?

رَبَّنَا لَا تُزِغْ قُلُوبَنَا بَعْدَ إِذْ هَدَيْتَنَا وَهَبْ لَنَا مِن لَّدُنكَ رَحْمَةً إِنَّكَ أَنتَ الْوَهَّابُ

"Our Lord! let not our hearts deviate after You have guided us, and bestow on us from Your mercy, for You are, indeed, the Ever-Bestower."
Surah al-Imran, verse 8

59

بِسْمِ اللَّهِ الرَّحْمَٰنِ الرَّحِيمِ

Date:_____   Day:_____

Ayah Tracker

Juz: _____

Surah: _____

Ayah No: _____

Progress Record

Studied: ☐

Memorised: ☐

Revised: ☐

Ayah:

Context:

Brief Commentary:

Source:

My Understanding:

words/meaning

How can I implement the lessons in my life?

رَبَّنَا هَبْ لَنَا مِنْ أَزْوَاجِنَا وَذُرِّيَّاتِنَا قُرَّةَ أَعْيُنٍ وَاجْعَلْنَا لِلْمُتَّقِينَ إِمَامًا

"Our Lord! grant unto us spouses and offspring who will be the comfort of our eyes and give us (the grace) to lead the righteous."
Surah Al Furqan, verse 74

ADDITIONAL NOTES:

بِسْمِ اللَّهِ الرَّحْمَنِ الرَّحِيمِ

Date:_____   Day:_____

Ayah Tracker

Juz: _____
Surah: _____
Ayah No: _____

Progress Record

Studied: ☐
Memorised: ☐
Revised: ☐

Ayah:

Context:

Brief Commentary:

Source:

My Understanding:

words/meaning

How can I implement the lessons in my life?

رَبَّنَا اصْرِفْ عَنَّا عَذَابَ جَهَنَّمَ ۖ إِنَّ عَذَابَهَا كَانَ غَرَامًا

"Our Lord, avert from us the punishment of Hell. Indeed, its punishment is ever adhering"
Surah Al Furqan, verse 65

65

بِسْمِ اللَّهِ الرَّحْمَٰنِ الرَّحِيمِ

Date:_____   Day:_____

Ayah Tracker

Juz: _____

Surah: _____

Ayah No: _____

Progress Record

Studied: ☐

Memorised: ☐

Revised: ☐

Ayah:

Context:

Brief Commentary:

Source:

My Understanding:

words/meaning

How can I implement the lessons in my life?

أَنِّي مَسَّنِيَ الضُّرُّ وَأَنتَ أَرْحَمُ الرَّاحِمِينَ

"Verily, distress has seized me, and You are the Most Merciful of all those who show mercy."
Surah Al Anbiya, verse 83

ADDITIONAL NOTES:

بِسْمِ اللَّهِ الرَّحْمَٰنِ الرَّحِيمِ

Date:_____   Day:_____

Ayah Tracker

Juz: _____
Surah: _____
Ayah No: _____

Progress Record

Studied: ☐
Memorised: ☐
Revised: ☐

Ayah:

Context:

Brief Commentary:

Source:

My Understanding:

words/meaning

How can I implement the lessons in my life?

رَبَّنَا آتِنَا مِن لَّدُنكَ رَحْمَةً وَهَيِّئْ لَنَا مِنْ أَمْرِنَا رَشَدًا

"Our Lord! Bestow on us mercy from Yourself, and facilitate for us our affair in the right way"
Surah Al Kahf, verse 10

Additional Notes:

بِسْمِ اللَّهِ الرَّحْمَنِ الرَّحِيمِ

Date:_____   Day:_____

Ayah Tracker

Juz: _____
Surah: _____
Ayah No: _____

Progress Record

Studied: ☐

Memorised: ☐

Revised: ☐

Ayah:

Context:

Brief Commentary:

Source:

My Understanding:

words/meaning

How can I implement the lessons in my life?

رَبِّ أَوْزِعْنِي أَنْ أَشْكُرَ نِعْمَتَكَ الَّتِي أَنْعَمْتَ عَلَيَّ وَعَلَى وَالِدَيَّ وَأَنْ أَعْمَلَ صَالِحًا تَرْضَاهُ وَأَدْخِلْنِي بِرَحْمَتِكَ فِي عِبَادِكَ الصَّالِحِينَ

"My Lord, enable me to be grateful for Your favor which You have bestowed upon me and upon my parents and to do righteousness of which You approve. And admit me by Your mercy into [the ranks of] Your righteous servants."
Surah An Naml, verse 19

ADDITIONAL NOTES:

بِسْمِ اللَّهِ الرَّحْمَنِ الرَّحِيمِ

Date: _____　　　　　　Day: _____

Ayah Tracker

Juz: _____
Surah: _____
Ayah No: _____

Progress Record

Studied: ☐
Memorised: ☐
Revised: ☐

Ayah:

Context:

Brief Commentary:

Source:

My Understanding:

words/meaning

How can I implement the lessons in my life?

رَبَّنَا آمَنَّا فَاكْتُبْنَا مَعَ الشَّاهِدِينَ

"Our Lord! we believe, so write us down with the witnesses (of truth)"
Surah Al Ma'ida, verse 83

ADDITIONAL NOTES:

بِسْمِ اللَّهِ الرَّحْمَنِ الرَّحِيمِ

Date: _____   Day: _____

Ayah Tracker

Juz: _____
Surah: _____
Ayah No: _____

Progress Record

Studied: ☐
Memorised: ☐
Revised: ☐

Ayah:

Context:

Brief Commentary:

Source:

My Understanding:

words/meaning

How can I implement the lessons in my life?

رَبَّنَا أَتْمِمْ لَنَا نُورَنَا وَاغْفِرْ لَنَا ۖ إِنَّكَ عَلَىٰ كُلِّ شَيْءٍ قَدِيرٌ

"Our Lord, complete our light for us and forgive us. Surely, You have power over all things"

Surah At Tahrim, verse 8

ADDITIONAL NOTES:

بِسْمِ اللَّهِ الرَّحْمَنِ الرَّحِيمِ

Date:_____   Day:_____

Ayah Tracker

Juz: _____
Surah: _____
Ayah No: _____

Progress Record
Studied: ☐
Memorised: ☐
Revised: ☐

Ayah:

Context:

Brief Commentary:

Source:

My Understanding:

words/meaning

How can I implement the lessons in my life?

رَّبِّ ارْحَمْهُمَا كَمَا رَبَّيَانِي صَغِيرًا

"O my Lord! have compassion on them, as they brought me up (when I was) little"

Surah Al Isra, verse 24

ADDITIONAL NOTES:

$$\text{بِسْمِ اللَّهِ الرَّحْمَـٰنِ الرَّحِيمِ}$$

Date: _____   Day: _____

Ayah Tracker

Juz: _____

Surah: _____

Ayah No: _____

Progress Record

Studied: ☐

Memorised: ☐

Revised: ☐

Ayah:

Context:

Brief Commentary:

Source:

My Understanding:

words/meaning

How can I implement the lessons in my life?

رَبِّ نَجِّنِي وَأَهْلِي مِمَّا يَعْمَلُونَ

"My Lord ! Save me and my family from (the consequence of) what they do."
Surah Ash Shu'ara, verse 169

ADDITIONAL NOTES:

بِسْمِ اللَّهِ الرَّحْمَنِ الرَّحِيمِ

Date: _____   Day: _____

Ayah Tracker

Juz: _____

Surah: _____

Ayah No: _____

Progress Record

Studied: ☐

Memorised: ☐

Revised: ☐

Ayah:

Context:

Brief Commentary:

Source:

My Understanding:

words/meaning

How can I implement the lessons in my life?

رَّبِّ أَدْخِلْنِي مُدْخَلَ صِدْقٍ وَأَخْرِجْنِي مُخْرَجَ صِدْقٍ وَاجْعَل لِّي مِن لَّدُنكَ سُلْطَانًا نَّصِيرًا

"My Lord, grant me an entrance of sincerity and an exit of sincerity, and grant me from Yourself a victorious power'
Surah Al Isra, verse 80

ADDITIONAL NOTES:

بِسْمِ اللَّهِ الرَّحْمَـٰنِ الرَّحِيمِ

Date:_____   Day:_____

Ayah Tracker

Juz: _____
Surah: _____
Ayah No: _____

Progress Record
Studied: ☐
Memorised: ☐
Revised: ☐

Ayah:

Context:

Brief Commentary:

Source:

My Understanding:

words/meaning

How can I implement the lessons in my life?

رَبِّ إِنِّي أَعُوذُ بِكَ أَنْ أَسْأَلَكَ مَا لَيْسَ لِي بِهِ عِلْمٌ وَإِلَّا تَغْفِرْ لِي وَتَرْحَمْنِي أَكُن مِّنَ الْخَاسِرِينَ

"My Lord, I seek refuge with You from asking You of that which I have no knowledge. If You do not forgive me and have mercy on me, I shall be among the losers."

Surah Hud, verse 47

ADDITIONAL NOTES:

بِسْمِ اللَّهِ الرَّحْمَنِ الرَّحِيمِ

Date: _____   Day: _____

Ayah Tracker

Juz: _____
Surah: _____
Ayah No: _____

Progress Record

Studied: ☐

Memorised: ☐

Revised: ☐

Ayah:

Context:

Brief Commentary:

Source:

My Understanding:

words/meaning

How can I implement the lessons in my life?

رَّبِّ اغْفِرْ لِي وَلِوَالِدَيَّ وَلِمَن دَخَلَ بَيْتِيَ مُؤْمِنًا وَلِلْمُؤْمِنِينَ وَالْمُؤْمِنَاتِ وَلَا تَزِدِ الظَّالِمِينَ إِلَّا تَبَارًا

"My Lord! forgive me and my parents and him who enters my house believing, and the believing men and the believing women; and do not increase the wrongdoer except in destruction "
Surah Nuh, verse 28

ADDITIONAL NOTES:

بِسْمِ اللَّهِ الرَّحْمَنِ الرَّحِيمِ

Date:_____   Day:_____

Ayah Tracker

Juz: _____

Surah: _____

Ayah No: _____

Progress Record

Studied: ☐

Memorised: ☐

Revised: ☐

Ayah:

Context:

Brief Commentary:

Source:

My Understanding:

words/meaning

How can I implement the lessons in my life?

الْحَمْدُ لِلَّهِ الَّذِي فَضَّلَنَا عَلَىٰ كَثِيرٍ مِّنْ عِبَادِهِ الْمُؤْمِنِينَ

"Praise be to Allah, Who has favoured us over many of His believing servants"
Surah An Naml, verse 15

ADDITIONAL NOTES:

WISDOM

وَالْقُرْآنِ الْحَكِيمِ

By the Qur'an, which is full of Wisdom
(36:2)

يُؤْتِى الْحِكْمَةَ مَنْ يَشَاءُ وَمَنْ يُؤْتَ الْحِكْمَةَ فَقَدْ أُوتِىَ خَيْرًا كَثِيرًا وَمَا يَذَّكَّرُ إِلَّا أُولُوا الْأَلْبَابِ

He gives wisdom to whom He wills, and whoever has been given wisdom
has certainly been given much good. And none will remember except those of
understanding.
(2:269)

Surah Study

Study Plan

1. Write the origin of the Surah.
2. Look into background history and textual context of the Surah.
3. Mention the central theme and other major themes discussed in the Surah.
4. Jot down the brief summary of the Surah in sub divided sections, according to the Ayahs and its message.
5. Learn the key words/phrases and write down the meanings.
6. Highlight the lessons from the Surah.

بِسْمِ اللَّهِ الرَّحْمَنِ الرَّحِيمِ

Date: _____   Day: _____

Surah: _____   Juzz: _____

Origin: Makki   Madni

Historical Background	Textual Context

Major   CENTRAL   THEME   Themes

Brief Summary
(sub-divided parts of surah)

Key words & Phrases

Lessons from the Surah:

ADDITIONAL NOTES:

بِسْمِ اللَّهِ الرَّحْمَنِ الرَّحِيمِ

Date: _____   Day: _____

Surah: _____   Juzz: _____

Origin: Makki   Madni

Historical Background	Textual Context

Major   CENTRAL   THEME   Themes

Brief Summary
(sub-divided parts of surah)

Key words & Phrases

Lessons from the Surah:

ADDITIONAL NOTES:

بِسْمِ اللَّهِ الرَّحْمَنِ الرَّحِيمِ

Date: Day:

Surah:_____   Juzz:_____

Origin: Makki   Madni

Historical Background	Textual Context

Major   CENTRAL   THEME   **Themes**

Brief Summary
(sub-divided parts of surah)

Key words & Phrases

Lessons from the Surah:

بِسْمِ اللَّهِ الرَّحْمَنِ الرَّحِيمِ

Date: Day:

Surah:_____   Juzz:_____

Origin: Makki   Madni

Historical Background

Textual Context

Major   CENTRAL THEME   Themes

Brief Summary
(sub-divided parts of surah)

Key words & Phrases

Lessons from the Surah:

ADDITIONAL NOTES:

ADDITIONAL NOTES:

بِسْمِ اللَّـهِ الرَّحْمَـٰنِ الرَّحِيمِ

Date: Day:

Surah:_____   Juzz:_____

Origin: Makki   Madni

Historical Background

Textual Context

Major   CENTRAL THEME   **Themes**

Brief Summary
(sub-divided parts of surah)

Key words & Phrases

Lessons from the Surah:

ADDITIONAL NOTES:

بِسْمِ اللَّهِ الرَّحْمَٰنِ الرَّحِيمِ

Date: Day:

Surah:_____   Juzz:_____

Origin: Makki   Madni

Historical Background

Textual Context

Major   CENTRAL THEME   Themes

Brief Summary (sub-divided parts of surah)	Key words & Phrases

Lessons from the Surah:

بِسْمِ اللَّهِ الرَّحْمَنِ الرَّحِيمِ

Date: _____ Day: _____

Surah: _____ Juzz: _____

Origin: Makki Madni

Historical Background

Textual Context

Major CENTRAL THEME Themes

Brief Summary
(sub-divided parts of surah)

Key words & Phrases

Lessons from the Surah:

Additional Notes:

بِسْمِ اللَّهِ الرَّحْمَنِ الرَّحِيمِ

Date: _____   Day: _____

Surah: _____   Juzz: _____

Origin: Makki   Madni

Historical Background	Textual Context

Major   CENTRAL THEME   Themes

Brief Summary
(sub-divided parts of surah)

Key words & Phrases

Lessons from the Surah:

ADDITIONAL NOTES:

بِسْمِ اللَّهِ الرَّحْمَٰنِ الرَّحِيمِ

Date: _____   Day: _____

Surah:_____   Juzz:_____

Origin: Makki   Madni

Historical Background

Textual Context

Major   CENTRAL THEME   **Themes**

Brief Summary
(sub-divided parts of surah)

Key words & Phrases

Lessons from the Surah:

ADDITIONAL NOTES:

بِسْمِ اللَّهِ الرَّحْمَنِ الرَّحِيمِ

Date: Day:

Surah:_____   Juzz:_____

Origin: Makki   Madni

Historical Background

Textual Context

Major

Themes

CENTRAL THEME

Brief Summary
(sub-divided parts of surah)

Key words & Phrases

Lessons from the Surah:

ADDITIONAL NOTES:

TRUTH

إِنَّا أَنزَلْنَا عَلَيْكَ الْكِتَابَ لِلنَّاسِ بِالْحَقِّ فَمَنِ اهْتَدَىٰ فَلِنَفْسِهِ ۖ وَمَن ضَلَّ فَإِنَّمَا يَضِلُّ عَلَيْهَا ۖ وَمَا أَنتَ عَلَيْهِم بِوَكِيلٍ

(O Prophet), We revealed to you the Book with the Truth for all mankind.
So he who follows the Right Way does so to his own benefit, and he who
goes astray, shall hurt only himself by straying. You are not accountable on
their behalf. (39:41)

المر ۚ تِلْكَ آيَاتُ الْكِتَابِ ۗ وَالَّذِي أُنزِلَ إِلَيْكَ مِن رَّبِّكَ الْحَقُّ وَلَٰكِنَّ أَكْثَرَ النَّاسِ لَا يُؤْمِنُونَ

Alif. Lam. Mim. Ra'. These are the verses of the Divine Book. Whatever
has been revealed to you from your Lord is the truth, and yet most (of
your) people do not believe. (13:1)

Overall Progress

Monthly Quran Review

Week 1
Week 2
Week 3
Week 4

Weekly Quran Review

Monday	
Tuesday	
Wednesday	
Thursday	
Friday	
Saturday	
Sunday	

Weekly Quran Review

Monday	
Tuesday	
Wednesday	
Thursday	
Friday	
Saturday	
Sunday	

Weekly Quran Review

Monday	
Tuesday	
Wednesday	
Thursday	
Friday	
Saturday	
Sunday	

Weekly Quran Review

Monday	
Tuesday	
Wednesday	
Thursday	
Friday	
Saturday	
Sunday	

New Vocabulary
Write the new words you learned

Word	Translation	Ayah No	Root

Word	Translation	Ayah No	Root

New Vocabulary
Write the new words you learned

Word	Translation	Ayah No	Root

Word	Translation	Ayah No	Root

New Vocabulary
Write the new words you learned

Word	Translation	Ayah No	Root

Word	Translation	Ayah No	Root

New Vocabulary
Write the new words you learned

Word	Translation	Ayah No	Root

Word	Translation	Ayah No	Root

New Vocabulary
Write the new words you learned

Word	Translation	Ayah No	Root

Word	Translation	Ayah No	Root

Quran Tracker

Mark your progress

Surah Al-Fatiha	No. of Ayahs						
	1	2	3	4	5	6	7

Surah Al-Baqarah	No. of Ayahs												
	1	2	3	4	5	6	7	8	9	10	11	12	13
	14	15	16	17	18	19	20	21	22	23	24	25	26
	27	28	29	30	31	32	33	34	35	36	37	38	39
	40	41	42	43	44	45	46	47	48	49	50	51	52
	53	54	55	56	57	58	59	60	61	62	63	64	65
	66	67	68	69	70	71	72	73	74	75	76	77	78
	79	80	81	82	83	84	85	86	87	88	89	90	91
	92	93	94	95	96	97	98	99	100	101	102	103	104
	105	106	107	108	109	110	111	112	113	114	115	116	117
	118	119	120	121	122	123	124	125	126	127	128	129	130
	131	132	133	134	135	136	137	138	139	140	141	142	143
	144	145	146	147	148	149	150	151	152	153	154	155	156
	157	158	159	160	161	162	163	164	165	166	167	168	169
	170	171	172	173	174	175	176	177	178	179	180	181	182
	183	184	185	186	187	188	189	190	191	192	193	194	195
	196	197	198	199	200	201	202	203	204	205	206	207	208
	209	210	211	212	213	214	215	216	217	218	219	220	221
	222	223	224	225	226	227	228	229	230	231	232	233	234
	235	236	237	238	239	240	241	242	243	244	245	246	247
	248	249	250	251	252	253	254	255	256	257	258	259	260
	261	262	263	264	265	266	267	268	269	270	271	272	273
	274	275	276	277	278	279	280	281	282	283	284	285	286

	1	2	3	4	5	6	7	8	9	10	11	12	13
	14	15	16	17	18	19	20	21	22	23	24	25	26
	27	28	29	30	31	32	33	34	35	36	37	38	39
	40	41	42	43	44	45	46	47	48	49	50	51	52
	53	54	55	56	57	58	59	60	61	62	63	64	65
	66	67	68	69	70	71	72	73	74	75	76	77	78
Surah Al-Imran	79	80	81	82	83	84	85	86	87	88	89	90	91
	92	93	94	95	96	97	98	99	100	101	102	103	104
	105	106	107	108	109	110	111	112	113	114	115	116	117
	118	119	120	121	122	123	124	125	126	127	128	129	130
	131	132	133	134	135	136	137	138	139	140	141	142	143
	144	145	146	147	148	149	150	151	152	153	154	155	156
	157	158	159	160	161	162	163	164	165	166	167	168	169
	170	171	172	173	174	175	176	177	178	179	180	181	182
	183	184	185	186	187	188	189	190	191	192	193	194	195
	196	197	198	199	200								

No. of Ayahs

	1	2	3	4	5	6	7	8	9	10	11	12	13
	14	15	16	17	18	19	20	21	22	23	24	25	26
	27	28	29	30	31	32	33	34	35	36	37	38	39
	40	41	42	43	44	45	46	47	48	49	50	51	52
	53	54	55	56	57	58	59	60	61	62	63	64	65
Surah An Nisa	66	67	68	69	70	71	72	73	74	75	76	77	78
	79	80	81	82	83	84	85	86	87	88	89	90	91
	92	93	94	95	96	97	98	99	100	101	102	103	104
	105	106	107	108	109	110	111	112	113	114	115	116	117
	118	119	120	121	122	123	124	125	126	127	128	129	130
	131	132	133	134	135	136	137	138	139	140	141	142	143
	144	145	146	147	148	149	150	151	152	153	154	155	156
	157	158	159	160	161	162	163	164	165	166	167	168	169
	170	171	172	173	174	175	176						

Surah Al Maida

1	2	3	4	5	6	7	8	9	10	11	12	13
14	15	16	17	18	19	20	21	22	23	24	25	26
27	28	29	30	31	32	33	34	35	36	37	38	39
40	41	42	43	44	45	46	47	48	49	50	51	52
53	54	55	56	57	58	59	60	61	62	63	64	65
66	67	68	69	70	71	72	73	74	75	76	77	78
79	80	81	82	83	84	85	86	87	88	89	90	91
92	93	94	95	96	97	98	99	100	101	102	103	104
105	106	107	108	109	110	111	112	113	114	115	116	117
118	119	120										

Surah Al An'am

1	2	3	4	5	6	7	8	9	10	11	12	13
14	15	16	17	18	19	20	21	22	23	24	25	26
27	28	29	30	31	32	33	34	35	36	37	38	39
40	41	42	43	44	45	46	47	48	49	50	51	52
53	54	55	56	57	58	59	60	61	62	63	64	65
66	67	68	69	70	71	72	73	74	75	76	77	78
79	80	81	82	83	84	85	86	87	88	89	90	91
92	93	94	95	96	97	98	99	100	101	102	103	104
105	106	107	108	109	110	111	112	113	114	115	116	117
118	119	120	121	122	123	124	125	126	127	128	129	130
131	132	133	134	135	136	137	138	139	140	141	142	143
144	145	146	147	148	149	150	151	152	153	154	155	156
157	158	159	160	161	162	163	164	165				

Surah Al A'raf

1	2	3	4	5	6	7	8	9	10	11	12	13
14	15	16	17	18	19	20	21	22	23	24	25	26
27	28	29	30	31	32	33	34	35	36	37	38	39
40	41	42	43	44	45	46	47	48	49	50	51	52
53	54	55	56	57	58	59	60	61	62	63	64	65
66	67	68	69	70	71	72	73	74	75	76	77	78

No. of Ayahs												
79	80	81	82	83	84	85	86	87	88	89	90	91
92	93	94	95	96	97	98	99	100	101	102	103	104
105	106	107	108	109	110	111	112	113	114	115	116	117
118	119	120	121	122	123	124	125	126	127	128	129	130
131	132	133	134	135	136	137	138	139	140	141	142	143
144	145	146	147	148	149	150	151	152	153	154	155	156
157	158	159	160	161	162	163	164	165	166	167	168	169
170	171	172	173	174	175	176	177	178	179	180	181	182
183	184	185	186	187	188	189	190	191	192	193	194	195
196	197	198	199	200	201	202	203	204	205	206		

Surah Al A'raf

No. of Ayahs												
1	2	3	4	5	6	7	8	9	10	11	12	13
14	15	16	17	18	19	20	21	22	23	24	25	26
27	28	29	30	31	32	33	34	35	36	37	38	39
40	41	42	43	44	45	46	47	48	49	50	51	52
53	54	55	56	57	58	59	60	61	62	63	64	65
66	67	68	69	70	71	72	73	74	75			

Surah Al Anfal

No. of Ayahs												
1	2	3	4	5	6	7	8	9	10	11	12	13
14	15	16	17	18	19	20	21	22	23	24	25	26
27	28	29	30	31	32	33	34	35	36	37	38	39
40	41	42	43	44	45	46	47	48	49	50	51	52
53	54	55	56	57	58	59	60	61	62	63	64	65
66	67	68	69	70	71	72	73	74	75	76	77	78
79	80	81	82	83	84	85	86	87	88	89	90	91
92	93	94	95	96	97	98	99	100	101	102	103	104
105	106	107	108	109	110	111	112	113	114	115	116	117
118	119	120	121	122	123	124	125	126	127	128	129	

Surah At Tawba

Surah Yunus

No. of Ayahs												
1	2	3	4	5	6	7	8	9	10	11	12	13
14	15	16	17	18	19	20	21	22	23	24	25	26
27	28	29	30	31	32	33	34	35	36	37	38	39
40	41	42	43	44	45	46	47	48	49	50	51	52
53	54	55	56	57	58	59	60	61	62	63	64	65
66	67	68	69	70	71	72	73	74	75	76	77	78
79	80	81	82	83	84	85	86	87	88	89	90	91
92	93	94	95	96	97	98	99	100	101	102	103	104
105	106	107	108	109								

Surah Hud

No. of Ayahs												
1	2	3	4	5	6	7	8	9	10	11	12	13
14	15	16	17	18	19	20	21	22	23	24	25	26
27	28	29	30	31	32	33	34	35	36	37	38	39
40	41	42	43	44	45	46	47	48	49	50	51	52
53	54	55	56	57	58	59	60	61	62	63	64	65
66	67	68	69	70	71	72	73	74	75	76	77	78
79	80	81	82	83	84	85	86	87	88	89	90	91
92	93	94	95	96	97	98	99	100	101	102	103	104
105	106	107	108	109	110	111	112	113	114	115	116	117
118	119	120	121	122	123							

Surah Yusuf

No. of Ayahs												
1	2	3	4	5	6	7	8	9	10	11	12	13
14	15	16	17	18	19	20	21	22	23	24	25	26
27	28	29	30	31	32	33	34	35	36	37	38	39
40	41	42	43	44	45	46	47	48	49	50	51	52
53	54	55	56	57	58	59	60	61	62	63	64	65
66	67	68	69	70	71	72	73	74	75	76	77	78
79	80	81	82	83	84	85	86	87	88	89	90	91
92	93	94	95	96	97	98	99	100	101	102	103	104
105	106	107	108	109	110	111						

Surah Ar Ra'd	No. of Ayahs												
	1	2	3	4	5	6	7	8	9	10	11	12	13
	14	15	16	17	18	19	20	21	22	23	24	25	26
	27	28	29	30	31	32	33	34	35	36	37	38	39
	40	41	42	43									

Surah Ibrahim	No. of Ayahs												
	1	2	3	4	5	6	7	8	9	10	11	12	13
	14	15	16	17	18	19	20	21	22	23	24	25	26
	27	28	29	30	31	32	33	34	35	36	37	38	39
	40	41	42	43	44	45	46	47	48	49	50	51	52

Surah Al Hijir	No. of Ayahs												
	1	2	3	4	5	6	7	8	9	10	11	12	13
	14	15	16	17	18	19	20	21	22	23	24	25	26
	27	28	29	30	31	32	33	34	35	36	37	38	39
	40	41	42	43	44	45	46	47	48	49	50	51	52
	53	54	55	56	57	58	59	60	61	62	63	64	65
	66	67	68	69	70	71	72	73	74	75	76	77	78
	79	80	81	82	83	84	85	86	87	88	89	90	91
	92	93	94	95	96	97	98	99					

Surah An Nahl	No. of Ayahs												
	1	2	3	4	5	6	7	8	9	10	11	12	13
	14	15	16	17	18	19	20	21	22	23	24	25	26
	27	28	29	30	31	32	33	34	35	36	37	38	39
	40	41	42	43	44	45	46	47	48	49	50	51	52
	53	54	55	56	57	58	59	60	61	62	63	64	65
	66	67	68	69	70	71	72	73	74	75	76	77	78
	79	80	81	82	83	84	85	86	87	88	89	90	91
	92	93	94	95	96	97	98	99	100	101	102	103	104
	105	106	107	108	109	110	111	112	113	114	115	116	117
	118	119	120	121	122	123	124	125	126	127	128		

Surah Al Isra

1	2	3	4	5	6	7	8	9	10	11	12	13
14	15	16	17	18	19	20	21	22	23	24	25	26
27	28	29	30	31	32	33	34	35	36	37	38	39
40	41	42	43	44	45	46	47	48	49	50	51	52
53	54	55	56	57	58	59	60	61	62	63	64	65
66	67	68	69	70	71	72	73	74	75	76	77	78
79	80	81	82	83	84	85	86	87	88	89	90	91
92	93	94	95	96	97	98	99	100	101	102	103	104
105	106	107	108	109	110	111						

Surah Al Kahf

1	2	3	4	5	6	7	8	9	10	11	12	13
14	15	16	17	18	19	20	21	22	23	24	25	26
27	28	29	30	31	32	33	34	35	36	37	38	39
40	41	42	43	44	45	46	47	48	49	50	51	52
53	54	55	56	57	58	59	60	61	62	63	64	65
66	67	68	69	70	71	72	73	74	75	76	77	78
79	80	81	82	83	84	85	86	87	88	89	90	91
92	93	94	95	96	97	98	99	100	101	102	103	104
105	106	107	108	109	110							

Surah Maryam

1	2	3	4	5	6	7	8	9	10	11	12	13
14	15	16	17	18	19	20	21	22	23	24	25	26
27	28	29	30	31	32	33	34	35	36	37	38	39
40	41	42	43	44	45	46	47	48	49	50	51	52
53	54	55	56	57	58	59	60	61	62	63	64	65
66	67	68	69	70	71	72	73	74	75	76	77	78
79	80	81	82	83	84	85	86	87	88	89	90	91
92	93	94	95	96	97	98						

Surah TaHa

1	2	3	4	5	6	7	8	9	10	11	12	13
14	15	16	17	18	19	20	21	22	23	24	25	26
27	28	29	30	31	32	33	34	35	36	37	38	39
40	41	42	43	44	45	46	47	48	49	50	51	52
53	54	55	56	57	58	59	60	61	62	63	64	65
66	67	68	69	70	71	72	73	74	75	76	77	78
79	80	81	82	83	84	85	86	87	88	89	90	91
92	93	94	95	96	97	98	99	100	101	102	103	104
105	106	107	108	109	110	111	112	113	114	115	116	117
118	119	120	121	122	123	124	125	126	127	128	129	130
131	132	133	134	135								

Surah Al Anbiya

1	2	3	4	5	6	7	8	9	10	11	12	13
14	15	16	17	18	19	20	21	22	23	24	25	26
27	28	29	30	31	32	33	34	35	36	37	38	39
40	41	42	43	44	45	46	47	48	49	50	51	52
53	54	55	56	57	58	59	60	61	62	63	64	65
66	67	68	69	70	71	72	73	74	75	76	77	78
79	80	81	82	83	84	85	86	87	88	89	90	91
92	93	94	95	96	97	98	99	100	101	102	103	104
105	106	107	108	109	110	111	112					

Surah Al Hajj

1	2	3	4	5	6	7	8	9	10	11	12	13
14	15	16	17	18	19	20	21	22	23	24	25	26
27	28	29	30	31	32	33	34	35	36	37	38	39
40	41	42	43	44	45	46	47	48	49	50	51	52
53	54	55	56	57	58	59	60	61	62	63	64	65
66	67	68	69	70	71	72	73	74	75	76	77	78

Surah Al Muminun

No. of Ayahs												
1	2	3	4	5	6	7	8	9	10	11	12	13
14	15	16	17	18	19	20	21	22	23	24	25	26
27	28	29	30	31	32	33	34	35	36	37	38	39
40	41	42	43	44	45	46	47	48	49	50	51	52
53	54	55	56	57	58	59	60	61	62	63	64	65
66	67	68	69	70	71	72	73	74	75	76	77	78
79	80	81	82	83	84	85	86	87	88	89	90	91
92	93	94	95	96	97	98	99	100	101	102	103	104
105	106	107	108	109	110	111	112	113	114	115	116	117
118												

Surah An Nur

No. of Ayahs												
1	2	3	4	5	6	7	8	9	10	11	12	13
14	15	16	17	18	19	20	21	22	23	24	25	26
27	28	29	30	31	32	33	34	35	36	37	38	39
40	41	42	43	44	45	46	47	48	49	50	51	52
53	54	55	56	57	58	59	60	61	62	63	64	

Surah Al Furqan

No. of Ayahs												
1	2	3	4	5	6	7	8	9	10	11	12	13
14	15	16	17	18	19	20	21	22	23	24	25	26
27	28	29	30	31	32	33	34	35	36	37	38	39
40	41	42	43	44	45	46	47	48	49	50	51	52
53	54	55	56	57	58	59	60	61	62	63	64	65
66	67	68	69	70	71	72	73	74	75	76	77	

Surah Ash Shu'ara

No. of Ayahs												
1	2	3	4	5	6	7	8	9	10	11	12	13
14	15	16	17	18	19	20	21	22	23	24	25	26
27	28	29	30	31	32	33	34	35	36	37	38	39
40	41	42	43	44	45	46	47	48	49	50	51	52
53	54	55	56	57	58	59	60	61	62	63	64	65
66	67	68	69	70	71	72	73	74	75	76	77	78
79	80	81	82	83	84	85	86	87	88	89	90	91
92	93	94	95	96	97	98	99	100	101	102	103	104
105	106	107	108	109	110	111	112	113	114	115	116	117
118	119	120	121	122	123	124	125	126	127	128	129	130
131	132	133	134	135	136	137	138	139	140	141	142	143
144	145	146	147	148	149	150	151	152	153	154	155	156
157	158	159	160	161	162	163	164	165	166	167	168	169
170	171	172	173	174	175	176	177	178	179	180	181	182
183	184	185	186	187	188	189	190	191	192	193	194	195
196	197	198	199	200	201	202	203	204	205	206	207	208
209	210	211	212	213	214	215	216	217	218	219	220	221
222	223	224	225	226	227							

Surah An Naml

No. of Ayahs												
1	2	3	4	5	6	7	8	9	10	11	12	13
14	15	16	17	18	19	20	21	22	23	24	25	26
27	28	29	30	31	32	33	34	35	36	37	38	39
40	41	42	43	44	45	46	47	48	49	50	51	52
53	54	55	56	57	58	59	60	61	62	63	64	65
66	67	68	69	70	71	72	73	74	75	76	77	78
79	80	81	82	83	84	85	86	87	88	89	90	91
92	93											

Surah Al Qasas

No. of Ayahs												
1	2	3	4	5	6	7	8	9	10	11	12	13
14	15	16	17	18	19	20	21	22	23	24	25	26
27	28	29	30	31	32	33	34	35	36	37	38	39
40	41	42	43	44	45	46	47	48	49	50	51	52
53	54	55	56	57	58	59	60	61	62	63	64	65
66	67	68	69	70	71	72	73	74	75	76	77	78
79	80	81	82	83	84	85	86	87	88			

Surah Al Ankabut

No. of Ayahs												
1	2	3	4	5	6	7	8	9	10	11	12	13
14	15	16	17	18	19	20	21	22	23	24	25	26
27	28	29	30	31	32	33	34	35	36	37	38	39
40	41	42	43	44	45	46	47	48	49	50	51	52
53	54	55	56	57	58	59	60	61	62	63	64	65
66	67	68	69									

Surah Ar Rum

No. of Ayahs												
1	2	3	4	5	6	7	8	9	10	11	12	13
14	15	16	17	18	19	20	21	22	23	24	25	26
27	28	29	30	31	32	33	34	35	36	37	38	39
40	41	42	43	44	45	46	47	48	49	50	51	52
53	54	55	56	57	58	59	60					

Surah Luqman

No. of Ayahs												
1	2	3	4	5	6	7	8	9	10	11	12	13
14	15	16	17	18	19	20	21	22	23	24	25	26
27	28	29	30	31	32	33	34					

Surah As Sajda

No. of Ayahs												
1	2	3	4	5	6	7	8	9	10	11	12	13
14	15	16	17	18	19	20	21	22	23	24	25	26
27	28	29	30									

Surah Al Ahzab

1	2	3	4	5	6	7	8	9	10	11	12	13
14	15	16	17	18	19	20	21	22	23	24	25	26
27	28	29	30	31	32	33	34	35	36	37	38	39
40	41	42	43	44	45	46	47	48	49	50	51	52
53	54	55	56	57	58	59	60	61	62	63	64	65
66	67	68	69	70	71	72	73					

Surah Saba

1	2	3	4	5	6	7	8	9	10	11	12	13
14	15	16	17	18	19	20	21	22	23	24	25	26
27	28	29	30	31	32	33	34	35	36	37	38	39
40	41	42	43	44	45	46	47	48	49	50	51	52
53	54											

Surah Fatir

1	2	3	4	5	6	7	8	9	10	11	12	13
14	15	16	17	18	19	20	21	22	23	24	25	26
27	28	29	30	31	32	33	34	35	36	37	38	39
40	41	42	43	44	45							

Surah Yaseen

1	2	3	4	5	6	7	8	9	10	11	12	13
14	15	16	17	18	19	20	21	22	23	24	25	26
27	28	29	30	31	32	33	34	35	36	37	38	39
40	41	42	43	44	45	46	47	48	49	50	51	52
53	54	55	56	57	58	59	60	61	62	63	64	65
66	67	68	69	70	71	72	73	74	75	76	77	78
79	80	81	82	83								

Surah As Saffat

1	2	3	4	5	6	7	8	9	10	11	12	13
14	15	16	17	18	19	20	21	22	23	24	25	26
27	28	29	30	31	32	33	34	35	36	37	38	39
40	41	42	43	44	45	46	47	48	49	50	51	52
53	54	55	56	57	58	59	60	61	62	63	64	65
66	67	68	69	70	71	72	73	74	75	76	77	78
79	80	81	82	83	84	85	86	87	88	89	90	91
92	93	94	95	96	97	98	99	100	101	102	103	104
105	106	107	108	109	110	111	112	113	114	115	116	117
118	119	120	121	122	123	124	125	126	127	128	129	130
131	132	133	134	135	136	137	138	139	140	141	142	143
144	145	146	147	148	149	150	151	152	153	154	155	156
157	158	159	160	161	162	163	164	165	166	167	168	169
170	171	172	173	174	175	176	177	178	179	180	181	182

Surah Sad

1	2	3	4	5	6	7	8	9	10	11	12	13
14	15	16	17	18	19	20	21	22	23	24	25	26
27	28	29	30	31	32	33	34	35	36	37	38	39
40	41	42	43	44	45	46	47	48	49	50	51	52
53	54	55	56	57	58	59	60	61	62	63	64	65
66	67	68	69	70	71	72	73	74	75	76	77	78
79	80	81	82	83	84	85	86	87	88			

Surah Az Zumar

1	2	3	4	5	6	7	8	9	10	11	12	13
14	15	16	17	18	19	20	21	22	23	24	25	26
27	28	29	30	31	32	33	34	35	36	37	38	39
40	41	42	43	44	45	46	47	48	49	50	51	52
53	54	55	56	57	58	59	60	61	62	63	64	65
66	67	68	69	70	71	72	73	74	75			

Surah Ghafir

No. of Ayahs												
1	2	3	4	5	6	7	8	9	10	11	12	13
14	15	16	17	18	19	20	21	22	23	24	25	26
27	28	29	30	31	32	33	34	35	36	37	38	39
40	41	42	43	44	45	46	47	48	49	50	51	52
53	54	55	56	57	58	59	60	61	62	63	64	65
66	67	68	69	70	71	72	73	74	75	76	77	78
79	80	81	82	83	84	85						

Surah Fussilat

No. of Ayahs												
1	2	3	4	5	6	7	8	9	10	11	12	13
14	15	16	17	18	19	20	21	22	23	24	25	26
27	28	29	30	31	32	33	34	35	36	37	38	39
40	41	42	43	44	45	46	47	48	49	50	51	52
53	54											

Surah Ash Shura

No. of Ayahs												
1	2	3	4	5	6	7	8	9	10	11	12	13
14	15	16	17	18	19	20	21	22	23	24	25	26
27	28	29	30	31	32	33	34	35	36	37	38	39
40	41	42	43	44	45	46	47	48	49	50	51	52
53												

Surah Az Zukhruf

No. of Ayahs												
1	2	3	4	5	6	7	8	9	10	11	12	13
14	15	16	17	18	19	20	21	22	23	24	25	26
27	28	29	30	31	32	33	34	35	36	37	38	39
40	41	42	43	44	45	46	47	48	49	50	51	52
53	54	55	56	57	58	59	60	61	62	63	64	65
66	67	68	69	70	71	72	73	74	75	76	77	78
79	80	81	82	83	84	85	86	87	88	89		

Surah Ad Dukhan

No. of Ayahs												
1	2	3	4	5	6	7	8	9	10	11	12	13
14	15	16	17	18	19	20	21	22	23	24	25	26
27	28	29	30	31	32	33	34	35	36	37	38	39
40	41	42	43	44	45	46	47	48	49	50	51	52
53	54	55	56	57	58	59						

Surah Jathiya

No. of Ayahs												
1	2	3	4	5	6	7	8	9	10	11	12	13
14	15	16	17	18	19	20	21	22	23	24	25	26
27	28	29	30	31	32	33	34	35	36	37		

Surah Al Ahqaf

No. of Ayahs												
1	2	3	4	5	6	7	8	9	10	11	12	13
14	15	16	17	18	19	20	21	22	23	24	25	26
27	28	29	30	31	32	33	34	35				

Surah Muhammad

No. of Ayahs												
1	2	3	4	5	6	7	8	9	10	11	12	13
14	15	16	17	18	19	20	21	22	23	24	25	26
27	28	29	30	31	32	33	34	35	36	37	38	

Surah Al Fath

No. of Ayahs												
1	2	3	4	5	6	7	8	9	10	11	12	13
14	15	16	17	18	19	20	21	22	23	24	25	26
27	28	29										

Surah Al Hujurat

No. of Ayahs												
1	2	3	4	5	6	7	8	9	10	11	12	13
14	15	16	17	18								

Surah Qaf

No. of Ayahs												
1	2	3	4	5	6	7	8	9	10	11	12	13
14	15	16	17	18	19	20	21	22	23	24	25	26
27	28	29	30	31	32	33	34	35	36	37	38	39
40	41	42	43	44	45							

Surah Ad Dhariyat

No. of Ayahs												
1	2	3	4	5	6	7	8	9	10	11	12	13
14	15	16	17	18	19	20	21	22	23	24	25	26
27	28	29	30	31	32	33	34	35	36	37	38	39
40	41	42	43	44	45	46	47	48	49	50	51	52
53	54	55	56	57	58	59	60					

Surah At Tur

No. of Ayahs												
1	2	3	4	5	6	7	8	9	10	11	12	13
14	15	16	17	18	19	20	21	22	23	24	25	26
27	28	29	30	31	32	33	34	35	36	37	38	39
40	41	42	43	44	45	46	47	48	49			

Surah An Najm

No. of Ayahs												
1	2	3	4	5	6	7	8	9	10	11	12	13
14	15	16	17	18	19	20	21	22	23	24	25	26
27	28	29	30	31	32	33	34	35	36	37	38	39
40	41	42	43	44	45	46	47	48	49	50	51	52
53	54	55	56	57	58	59	60	61	62			

Surah Al Qamar

No. of Ayahs												
1	2	3	4	5	6	7	8	9	10	11	12	13
14	15	16	17	18	19	20	21	22	23	24	25	26
27	28	29	30	31	32	33	34	35	36	37	38	39
40	41	42	43	44	45	46	47	48	49	50	51	52
53	54	55										

Surah Ar Rahman

No. of Ayahs												
1	2	3	4	5	6	7	8	9	10	11	12	13
14	15	16	17	18	19	20	21	22	23	24	25	26
27	28	29	30	31	32	33	34	35	36	37	38	39
40	41	42	43	44	45	46	47	48	49	50	51	52
53	54	55	56	57	58	59	60	61	62	63	64	65
66	67	68	69	70	71	72	73	74	75	76	77	78

Surah Al Waqi'a

No. of Ayahs												
1	2	3	4	5	6	7	8	9	10	11	12	13
14	15	16	17	18	19	20	21	22	23	24	25	26
27	28	29	30	31	32	33	34	35	36	37	38	39
40	41	42	43	44	45	46	47	48	49	50	51	52
53	54	55	56	57	58	59	60	61	62	63	64	65
66	67	68	69	70	71	72	73	74	75	76	77	78
79	80	81	82	83	84	85	86	87	88	89	90	91
92	93	94	95	96								

Surah Al Hadid

No. of Ayahs												
1	2	3	4	5	6	7	8	9	10	11	12	13
14	15	16	17	18	19	20	21	22	23	24	25	26
27	28	29										

Surah Al Mujadila

No. of Ayahs												
1	2	3	4	5	6	7	8	9	10	11	12	13
14	15	16	17	18	19	20	21	22				

Surah Al Hashr

No. of Ayahs												
1	2	3	4	5	6	7	8	9	10	11	12	13
14	15	16	17	18	19	20	21	22	23	24		

Surah Al Mumtahina

No. of Ayahs												
1	2	3	4	5	6	7	8	9	10	11	12	13

Surah As Saff

No. of Ayahs												
1	2	3	4	5	6	7	8	9	10	11	12	13
14												

Surah Al Jumu'a

No. of Ayahs										
1	2	3	4	5	6	7	8	9	10	11

Surah Al Munafiqun

No. of Ayahs										
1	2	3	4	5	6	7	8	9	10	11

Surah At Taghabun	No. of Ayahs												
	1	2	3	4	5	6	7	8	9	10	11	12	13
	14	15	16	17	18								

Surah At Talaq	No. of Ayahs												
	1	2	3	4	5	6	7	8	9	10	11	12	

Surah At Tahrim	No. of Ayahs												
	1	2	3	4	5	6	7	8	9	10	11	12	

Surah Al Mulk	No. of Ayahs												
	1	2	3	4	5	6	7	8	9	10	11	12	13
	14	15	16	17	18	19	20	21	22	23	24	25	26
	27	28	29	30									

Surah Al Qalam	No. of Ayahs												
	1	2	3	4	5	6	7	8	9	10	11	12	13
	14	15	16	17	18	19	20	21	22	23	24	25	26
	27	28	29	30	31	32	33	34	35	36	37	38	39
	40	41	42	43	44	45	46	47	48	49	50	51	52

Surah Al Haqqa	No. of Ayahs												
	1	2	3	4	5	6	7	8	9	10	11	12	13
	14	15	16	17	18	19	20	21	22	23	24	25	26
	27	28	29	30	31	32	33	34	35	36	37	38	39
	40	41	42	43	44	45	46	47	48	49	50	51	52

Surah Al Ma'arij	No. of Ayahs												
	1	2	3	4	5	6	7	8	9	10	11	12	13
	14	15	16	17	18	19	20	21	22	23	24	25	26
	27	28	29	30	31	32	33	34	35	36	37	38	39
	40	41	42	43	44								

Surah Nuh	No. of Ayahs												
	1	2	3	4	5	6	7	8	9	10	11	12	13
	14	15	16	17	18	19	20	21	22	23	24	25	26
	27	28											

Surah Al Jinn	No. of Ayahs												
	1	2	3	4	5	6	7	8	9	10	11	12	13
	14	15	16	17	18	19	20	21	22	23	24	25	26
	27	28											

Surah Al Muzzammil	No. of Ayahs												
	1	2	3	4	5	6	7	8	9	10	11	12	13
	14	15	16	17	18	19	20						

Surah Al Muddathir	No. of Ayahs												
	1	2	3	4	5	6	7	8	9	10	11	12	13
	14	15	16	17	18	19	20	21	22	23	24	25	26
	27	28	29	30	31	32	33	34	35	36	37	38	39
	40	41	42	43	44	45	46	47	48	49	50	51	52
	53	54	55	56									

Surah Al Qiyama	No. of Ayahs												
	1	2	3	4	5	6	7	8	9	10	11	12	13
	14	15	16	17	18	19	20	21	22	23	24	25	26
	27	28	29	30	31	32	33	34	35	36	37	38	39
	40												

Surah Al Insan	No. of Ayahs												
	1	2	3	4	5	6	7	8	9	10	11	12	13
	14	15	16	17	18	19	20	21	22	23	24	25	26
	27	28	29	30	31								

Surah Al Mursalat	No. of Ayahs												
	1	2	3	4	5	6	7	8	9	10	11	12	13
	14	15	16	17	18	19	20	21	22	23	24	25	26
	27	28	29	30	31	32	33	34	35	36	37	38	39
	40	41	42	43	44	45	46	47	48	49	50		

Surah An Naba

No. of Ayahs												
1	2	3	4	5	6	7	8	9	10	11	12	13
14	15	16	17	18	19	20	21	22	23	24	25	26
27	28	29	30	31	32	33	34	35	36	37	38	39
40												

Surah An Naziat

No. of Ayahs												
1	2	3	4	5	6	7	8	9	10	11	12	13
14	15	16	17	18	19	20	21	22	23	24	25	26
27	28	29	30	31	32	33	34	35	36	37	38	39
40	41	42	43	44	45	46						

Surah Abasa

No. of Ayahs												
1	2	3	4	5	6	7	8	9	10	11	12	13
14	15	16	17	18	19	20	21	22	23	24	25	26
27	28	29	30	31	32	33	34	35	36	37	38	39
40	41	42										

Surah At Takwir

No. of Ayahs												
1	2	3	4	5	6	7	8	9	10	11	12	13
14	15	16	17	18	19	20	21	22	23	24	25	26
27	28	29										

Surah Al Infitar

No. of Ayahs												
1	2	3	4	5	6	7	8	9	10	11	12	13
14	15	16	17	18	19							

Surah Al Mutaffiffin

No. of Ayahs												
1	2	3	4	5	6	7	8	9	10	11	12	13
14	15	16	17	18	19	20	21	22	23	24	25	26
27	28	29	30	31	32	33	34	35	36			

Surah Al Inshiqaq

No. of Ayahs												
1	2	3	4	5	6	7	8	9	10	11	12	13
14	15	16	17	18	19	20	21	22	23	24	25	

Surah Al Buruj	No. of Ayahs												
	1	2	3	4	5	6	7	8	9	10	11	12	13
	14	15	16	17	18	19	20	21	22				

Surah At Tariq	No. of Ayahs												
	1	2	3	4	5	6	7	8	9	10	11	12	13
	14	15	16	17									

Surah Al A'la	No. of Ayahs												
	1	2	3	4	5	6	7	8	9	10	11	12	13
	14	15	16	17	18	19							

Surah Al Ghashiya	No. of Ayahs												
	1	2	3	4	5	6	7	8	9	10	11	12	13
	14	15	16	17	18	19	20	21	22	23	24	25	26

Surah Al Fajr	No. of Ayahs												
	1	2	3	4	5	6	7	8	9	10	11	12	13
	14	15	16	17	18	19	20	21	22	23	24	25	26
	27	28	29	30									

Surah Al Balad	No. of Ayahs												
	1	2	3	4	5	6	7	8	9	10	11	12	13
	14	15	16	17	18	19	20						

Surah Ash Shams	No. of Ayahs												
	1	2	3	4	5	6	7	8	9	10	11	12	13
	14	15											

Surah Al Lail	No. of Ayahs												
	1	2	3	4	5	6	7	8	9	10	11	12	13
	14	15	16	17	18	19	20	21					

Surah Ad Dhuha	No. of Ayahs												
	1	2	3	4	5	6	7	8	9	10	11		

Surah Ash Sharh	No. of Ayahs												
	1	2	3	4	5	6	7	8					

Surah At Tin	No. of Ayahs												
	1	2	3	4	5	6	7	8					

Surah Al Alaq	No. of Ayahs												
	1	2	3	4	5	6	7	8	9	10	11	12	13
	14	15	16	17	18	19							

Surah Al Qadr	No. of Ayahs				
	1	2	3	4	5

Surah Al Bayyina	No. of Ayahs							
	1	2	3	4	5	6	7	8

Surah Az Zalzala	No. of Ayahs							
	1	2	3	4	5	6	7	8

Surah Al Adiyat	No. of Ayahs										
	1	2	3	4	5	6	7	8	9	10	11

Surah Al Qari'a	No. of Ayahs										
	1	2	3	4	5	6	7	8	9	10	11

Surah At Takathur	No. of Ayahs							
	1	2	3	4	5	6	7	8

Surah Al Asr	No. of Ayahs		
	1	2	3

Surah Al Humaza	No. of Ayahs								
	1	2	3	4	5	6	7	8	9

Surah Al fil	No. of Ayahs				
	1	2	3	4	5

Surah Quraysh	No. of Ayahs			
	1	2	3	4

Surah Al Ma'un	No. of Ayahs						
	1	2	3	4	5	6	7

Surah Al Kawthar	No. of Ayahs							
	1	2	3					

Surah Al Kafirun	No. of Ayahs							
	1	2	3	4	5	6		

Surah An Nasr	No. of Ayahs							
	1	2	3					

Surah Al Masad	No. of Ayahs							
	1	2	3	4	5			

Surah Al Ikhlas	No. of Ayahs							
	1	2	3	4				

Surah Al Falaq	No. of Ayahs							
	1	2	3	4	5			

Surah An Nas	No. of Ayahs							
	1	2	3	4	5	6		

وَهَـٰذَا كِتَابٌ أَنزَلْنَاهُ مُبَارَكٌ فَاتَّبِعُوهُ وَاتَّقُوا الْعَلَّكُمْ تُرْحَمُونَ

And this [Qur'an] is a Book We have revealed [which is] blessed,
so follow it and fear Allah that you may receive mercy.

Surah Al An'am, verse 155

CPSIA information can be obtained
at www.ICGtesting.com
Printed in the USA
LVHW07n1843260318
571185LV00009B/160/P